Wolves

Photographs by Art Wolfe

A BOOK OF POSTCARDS

Pomegranate Artbooks
San Francisco

Pomegranate Artbooks
Box 6099
Rohnert Park, CA 94927

ISBN 0-87654-099-X
Pomegranate Catalog No. A756

Pomegranate publishes books of postcards on a wide range of subjects.
Please write to the publisher for more information.

Designed by Tom Morley
Printed in Korea

*T*he images that come to mind when we hear the word *wolf* are strong ones: a frosty night lit by a full moon and made eerie by plaintive howling; a circling pack of toothy, doglike animals moving in for the kill; a lone beast gazing knowingly from the depths of a forest. But these are the images of popular culture and fairy tales, and they are far from the whole story.

In fact, wolves in the wild are shy, intelligent animals with a highly structured and closely knit social order. The basic unit of wolf society is the pack—an "alpha" (dominant) pair and their young, along with a few close relatives. Group cohesion is ensured by a precisely defined hierarchy maintained by intricate displays of posture, gaze and vocalization; for example, challenge barks and growls by higher-ranking wolves are met with submissive whines by those of lower rank. But wolves' vocal repertoire extends far beyond the language of dominance, including alarm barks, whimpers of greeting or of concern over a missing pup, squeaks by parents to retrieve or calm wayward youngsters—and, of course, the hallmark of the species, the howl, which may call the pack together before or after a hunt (a deep, single howl followed by a few barks) or indicate that an individual has been left behind (a plaintive howl starting on a high note, then quickly dropping in pitch). More than anything, though, howling seems to be a social activity undertaken for sheer enjoyment. A single wolf begins and the rest of the pack is irresistibly drawn in, forming a chorus of widely varying notes—the better to sound like a pack twice the size.

Perhaps the most appealing feature of pack life is wolves' devotion to their young. When pups are about three months old, they are moved from their underground den to a "rendezvous site," a grassy, open area about half an acre in size and bordered by trees or swamps. Pack life revolves around the rendezvous site for two or three months as the pups enjoy a golden summer of play and affection, being fed and cared for by all members of the pack. It is during this time that dominance among the pups begins to be established through their play, but the frolicking is not limited to the young. Adults spend a great deal of time joining in the merriment, and even elder dignitaries endure the pups' mischievous advances with apparent pleasure. Interestingly, there have even been accounts of wolves caring for other species' young. Some fifty cases of wolves caring for human children have been documented in India, and international news reports in 1978 told of a lost child in the Soviet Union who, when found, told her mother, "A big dog took care of me, and kept licking my face." Researchers located the "big dog"—it was a wolf.

For decades scientists have been fascinated by "lone wolves," possibly low-ranking wolves who have been pushed out of the pack or dominant wolves who have chosen not to challenge the pack's alpha. Whatever their origin, they, too, contribute to the wolf community. A lone wolf may travel hundreds of miles to begin a new pack with another lone wolf, thus revitalizing the blood line and promoting the species' survival.

As we continue to study the ways of the wolf, hoping to discover further keys to its preservation, the facts about this intriguing animal are proving to be more compelling than the myths. In this book of postcards renowned nature photographer Art Wolfe offers us a rare glimpse into the world of the wolf and explores the many facets of this beautiful, enigmatic creature.

Wolves

Photograph by Art Wolfe
Maned wolves (*Chrysocyon brachyurus*)

POMEGRANATE BOX 6099 ROHNERT PARK CA 94927

Wolves

Photograph by Art Wolfe
Maned wolves (*Chrysocyon brachyurus*)

POMEGRANATE BOX 6099 ROHNERT PARK CA 94927

Wolves

Photograph by Art Wolfe
Eight-week-old gray wolf pups and mom (*Canis lupus*)

POMEGRANATE   BOX 6099   ROHNERT PARK, CA 94927

Wolves

Photograph by Art Wolfe
Gray wolves (*Canis lupus*)

POMEGRANATE BOX 6099 ROHNERT PARK CA 94927

Wolves

Photograph by Art Wolfe
Mexican wolf (*Canis lupus baileyi*)

POMEGRANATE BOX 6099 ROHNERT PARK CA 94927

Wolves

Photograph by Art Wolfe
Arctic wolf

POMEGRANATE   BOX 6099   ROHNERT PARK, CA 94927

Wolves

Photograph by Art Wolfe
Arctic wolf

Pomegranate   Box 6099   Rohnert Park CA 94927

Wolves

Photograph by Art Wolfe
Gray wolf (*Canis lupus*)

Pomegranate Box 6099 Rohnert Park, CA 94927

Wolves

Photograph by Art Wolfe
Eight-week-old gray wolf pup and mom (*Canis lupus*)

POMEGRANATE BOX 6099 ROHNERT PARK CA 94927

Wolves

Photograph by Art Wolfe
Eight-week-old gray wolf pups and mom (*Canis lupus*)

POMEGRANATE   BOX 6099   ROHNERT PARK CA 94927

Wolves

Photograph by Art Wolfe
Red wolf (*Canis rufus*)

Pomegranate   Box 6099   Rohnert Park   CA   94927

Wolves

Photograph by Art Wolfe
Gray wolves (*Canis lupus*)

Pomegranate   Box 6099   Rohnert Park, CA 94927

Wolves

Photograph by Art Wolfe
Gray wolf (*Canis lupus*)

POMEGRANATE   BOX 6099   ROHNERT PARK, CA 94927

Wolves

Photograph by Art Wolfe
Gray wolf pups at den (*Canis lupus*)

Pomegranate   Box 6099   Rohnert Park CA 94927

Wolves

Photograph by Art Wolfe
Gray wolf (*Canis lupus*)

POMEGRANATE   BOX 6099   ROHNERT PARK CA 94927

Wolves

Photograph by Art Wolfe
Arctic wolf

POMEGRANATE   BOX 6099   ROHNERT PARK CA 94927

Wolves

Photograph by Art Wolfe
Gray wolf (*Canis lupus*)

POMEGRANATE BOX 6099 ROHNERT PARK, CA 94927

Wolves

Photograph by Art Wolfe
Gray wolf (*Canis lupus*)

Pomegranate Box 6099 Rohnert Park CA 94927

Wolves

Photograph by Art Wolfe
Eight-week-old gray wolf pup (*Canis lupus*)

POMEGRANATE   BOX 6099   ROHNERT PARK CA 94927

Wolves

Photograph by Art Wolfe
Maned wolf (*Chrysocyon brachyurus*)

POMEGRANATE   BOX 6099   ROHNERT PARK CA 94927

Wolves

Photograph by Art Wolfe
Mexican wolf (*Canis lupus baileyi*)

Pomegranate   Box 6099   Rohnert Park CA 94927

Wolves

Photograph by Art Wolfe
Arctic wolf

Pomegranate   Box 6099   Rohnert Park CA 94927

Wolves

Photograph by Art Wolfe
Red wolf (*Canis rufus*)

Pomegranate Box 6099 Rohnert Park CA 94927

Wolves

Photograph by Art Wolfe
Gray wolves (*Canis lupus*)

POMEGRANATE BOX 6099 ROHNERT PARK CA 94927

Wolves

Photograph by Art Wolfe
Eight-week-old gray wolf pups (*Canis lupus*)

Pomegranate Box 6099 Rohnert Park CA 94927

Wolves

Photograph by Art Wolfe
Eight-week-old gray wolf pup and mom (*Canis lupus*)

POMEGRANATE   BOX 6099   ROHNERT PARK CA 94927

Wolves

Photograph by Art Wolfe
Gray wolf (*Canis lupus*) at beaver dam

POMEGRANATE   BOX 6099   ROHNERT PARK CA 94927

Wolves

Photograph by Art Wolfe
Gray wolf (*Canis lupus*)

POMEGRANATE BOX 6099 ROHNERT PARK CA 94927

Wolves

Photograph by Art Wolfe
Gray wolf (*Canis lupus*)

POMEGRANATE · BOX 6099 · ROHNERT PARK · CA · 94927

Wolves

Photograph by Art Wolfe
Gray wolf (*Canis lupus*)

Pomegranate   Box 6099   Rohnert Park CA 94927